MW00965337

Sophia's Recipes:

Dessert book

Sophia moody

Copyright © 2020 Sophia Moody

All rights reserved

Sommario

Biscuit based cheesecake

Preparation: 40 min, ready in 1 h 20 min

Nutritional values

- *Calories 418 kcal (20%)*
- *Protein 16 g (16%)*
- *Fat 27 g (23%)*
- *Carbohydrates 28 g (19%)*
- *added sugar 17 g (68%)*
- *Fibre 4.4 g (15%)*

Ingredients

- 150 g whole grain biscuit
- 50 g butter
- 1 tbsp beet syrup
- 500 g ricotta
- 300 g low-fat quark
- 2 eggs
- 2 tbsp food starch
- ½ tsp vanilla powder
- 50 g raw cane sugar
- 100 g chopped almond
- 150 g small candy bars
- 150 ml whipped cream

Preparation steps

1. Place the biscuits in a clean tea towel and use the pin to crush them into crumbs. Melt butter over low heat in a small saucepan and mix with crumbs and beet syrup. Line the baker's springform pan. Pour the biscuit mixture and press firmly.

2. Combine ricotta and quark. Gradually add eggs, cornstarch whisk, vanilla and sugar. Fold the cream's almonds. Place the bars on the cake base and smooth the cream over them. Bake 50–60 minutes in a preheated oven (convection 160°C; gas: level 2–3).

3. Take the cheesecake off the oven and let it cool in the pan. Remove the cheesecake and let it cool down completely.

Whip until stiff and serve with cake.

Preparation: 10 min

Nutritional values

- *Calories 311 kcal (15%)*
- *Protein 12 g (12%)*
- *Fat 7 g (6%)*
- *Carbohydrates 48 g (32%)*
- *added sugar 13 g (52%)*
- *Fibre 3.5 g (12%)*

Ingredients

- *40 g ladyfingers (6 ladyfingers)*
- *2 tbsp passion fruit juice*
- *75 g strawberries (6 strawberries)*
- *2 tbsp yogurt (1.5% fat)*

- 1 tbsp lowfat quark
- 2 half apricots (can)
- 1 tsp pistachios
- 1 tsp honey

Preparation steps

1. Spread the ladyfingers in a small flat bowl and drizzle evenly with the passion fruit juice.
2. Clean and wash the strawberries and put 1 nice berry aside. Cut the rest of the berries into small cubes and sprinkle over the ladyfingers.
3. Stir yoghurt and quark in a small bowl until creamy. Distribute strawberries evenly.
4. Drain the apricot halves into narrow wedges.
5. Chop pistachios roughly.

Place the strawberry in the middle of the layered dish, and arrange the apricot wedges around it like flower petals. Sprinkle with pistachios, honey and serve.

Preparation: 50 min, ready in 5 h 40 min

Ingredients

For the dough

- *300 g flour and flour to work with*
- *100 g sugar*
- *1 pinch salt*
- *200 g butter*
- *1 egg*
- *dried pulses for blind baking*

For the caramel layer

- *600 ml whipped cream*
- *300 g sugar*

- *75 g butter*
- *75 ml whiskey cream liqueur*
- *400 g dark chocolate couverture*

For the chocolate layer

- *400 g dark chocolate couverture*

Preparation steps

1. *Put the flour on the work surface and form a hollow middle. Spread the sugar, salt, and butter on the flour edge. Put the egg in the middle and chop the crumbs with a pastry card. Knead with your hands to form a smooth dough no longer sticking to your hands. Wrap in film and put in fridge for about 30 minutes.*

2. *Preheat fan oven to 180°C. Line a deep parchment-paper baking sheet.*

3. *Roll out the dough to a sheet size on a floured surface and place on the baking sheet. With a fork, pinch the bottom several times, cover with baking paper and legumes. Bake for 15-20 minutes until golden. Remove the legumes and paper and let cool on the baking sheet.*

4. *Cook cream, sugar, butter and liqueur in a saucepan for the caramel layer while stirring over low heat for about 30 minutes,*

stirring occasionally (up to about 1/3) until golden yellow and thick. Remove from heat, stir in chopped chocolate and let cool down.

5. Put the mixture on the floor and smooth. Let it cool down for about 2 hours.

6. Chop the cover to coat, melt over a hot water bath and let cool down. Smooth on the caramel layer, set for about 1 hour.

7. Serve in pieces.

Preparation: 30 min, ready in 52 min

Nutritional values

- *Calories 283 kcal (13%)*
- *Protein 6 g (6%)*
- *Fat 20 g (17%)*
- *Carbohydrates 21 g (14%)*
- *added sugar 19 g (76%)*
- *Fiber 4.3 g (14%)*

Ingredients

- 175 g biscuit z. b. whole grain or shortbread biscuits
- 200 g roasted almond kernels
- 75 g brown sugar
- 150 g melted butter
- 400 g coconut flakes
- 350 g sweetened condensed milk
- 500 g dark chocolate couverture

Preparation steps

1. Preheat the oven to 175 ° C lower and upper heat.
2. The base coarsely crumble the biscuits and finely crumble them with 75 g almonds and the sugar in a lightning chopper. Mix in the butter and press evenly flat in a baking pan lined with baking paper (approx. 32x24 cm). Bake in the oven for about 20 minutes.
3. Mix the coconut flakes with the condensed milk. Take the bottom out of the oven and spread the coconut mixture on top. Sprinkle with the remaining almonds and bake in the oven for another 10 minutes. Then take it out of the oven again.
4. Chop the chocolate and let it melt over a hot water bath. Let it cool down a little, spread it on the cake and let it cool down on a wire rack (in the fridge if necessary).
5. Cut into pieces before serving.

Cream slices with raspberries

Ingredients

- 250 g raspberries
- 2 sheets gelatin
- 2 tbsp raspberry liqueur
- 150 g mascarpone
- 200 g whipped cream
- 3 tbsp cane sugar
- 1 packet vanilla sugar
- 1 packet cream stiffener
- 6 nut and granola bars
- lemon balm for garnish

Preparation steps

1. Wash and sort the berries. Puree approx. 1/4 of it and strain through a sieve. Soak the gelatine in cold water. Then squeeze out and dissolve in warm liqueur. Stir into the puree.

2. Mix the mascarpone until smooth with the sugar and vanilla sugar, whip the cream until stiff with the cream stiffener and fold in the mascarpone, then stir in the raspberry puree.

3. Put together the muesli bars with their long sides and frame them with aluminium foil (approx. 5 cm high). On the muesli platter, spread 3/4 of the cream, pour the raspberry puree on top, and spread the remainder of the cream on top. Min. Min. Just chill for two hours. Cut into 6 slices with a hot knife (dip in hot water briefly) and garnish with the remaining berries and lemon balm to serve.

Healthy hot chocolate

Nutritional values

- *Calories 150 kcal (7%)*
- *Protein 11 g (11%)*
- *Fat 3 g (3%)*
- *Carbohydrates 18 g (12%)*
- *added sugar 0 g (0%)*
- *Fiber 6.6 g (22%)*

Ingredients

- *1 ½ tsp cocoa powder*
- *1 pinch cinnamon*
- *2 pitted soft dates*
- *250 ml almond drink (almond milk) or another plant-based milk alternative*
- *cocoa nibs or vegan spray cream as desired*

Preparation steps

1. *Crush the cocoa with cinnamon, soft dates (2 or 3 depending on the desired sweetness) and plant-based milk of your choice with a hand blender until the dates are finely pureed.*
2. *Slowly heat the mixture in a saucepan.*
3. *Pour into a cup and top the hot chocolate with (vegan) spray cream, cocoa nibs and some cocoa powder if you like.*

Spicy hot chocolate

Nutritional values

- *Calories 239 kcal (11%)*
- *Protein 10 g (10%)*
- *Fat 12 g (10%)*
- *Carbohydrates 22 g (15%)*
- *added sugar 4 g (16%)*
- *Fiber 6 g (20%)*

ingredients

- *5 g chilli pepper*
- *30 g ginger in one piece*
- *1 vanilla pod*
- *70 g dark chocolate (at least 70% cocoa content, vegan)*
- *400 ml almond drink (almond milk)*

- 2 cinnamon sticks
- 3-star anise
- cinnamon powder

Preparation steps

1. Wash the chilli pepper and ginger and cut into small pieces. Halve the vanilla pod, scrape out the pulp and set aside. Roughly chop the chocolate and also set aside.
2. Put the almond drink with chilli, ginger, scraped vanilla pod, cinnamon sticks and star anise in a saucepan and heat. Cover and let simmer over low heat for about 10 minutes.
3. Pour the spiced drink through a sieve into a bowl and reheat the liquid in the pot. Stir in vanilla pulp and chopped chocolate and let melt.
4. Divide the Spicy Hot Chocolate between two mugs, sprinkle with cinnamon and enjoy hot.

Coconut cream cake with chocolate base

Nutritional values

- *Calories 389 kcal (19%)*
- *Protein 7 g (7%)*
- *Fat 26 g (22%)*
- *Carbohydrates 33 g (22%)*
- *added sugar 9 g (36%)*
- *Fibre 2.9 g (10%)*

Ingredients

- *2 eggs*
- *1 pinch salt*
- *80 g agave syrup*

- 125 g butter
- 220 g wheat flour type 1050 or spelled flour 1050
- ½ packet baking powder
- 30 g cocoa powder (heavily de-oiled)
- 1 packet vanilla pudding powder
- 400 ml coconut milk (9% fat)
- 30 g coconut blossom sugar
- 40 g coconut flakes
- 4 sheets gelatin
- 150 ml whipped cream
- 100 g dark chocolate
- 20 g coconut oil

Preparation steps

1. Separate the eggs and beat the egg whites with salt to form egg whites. Mix agave syrup with butter and egg yolk until frothy. Mix the flour, baking powder and cocoa and sift into the egg yolk foam, then work into a smooth dough and very carefully fold in the egg whites.

2. Line the springform pan with baking paper or grease. Pour in the dough, smooth it out and bake at 180 ° C (convection 160 ° C; gas: level 2) for about 25-30 minutes (make a stick test). Then let the cake cool in the pan.

3. In the meantime, stir the pudding powder with 5–6 tablespoons of coconut milk until smooth. Put the remaining coconut milk, coconut blossom sugar and 30 g coconut flakes in a saucepan and bring to the boil. Stir in the mixed pudding powder, bring to the boil while stirring and then allow to cool.

4. *Soak the gelatine in cold water. Whip 100 ml cream until stiff. Slightly heat the rest of the cream in a saucepan and dissolve the well-squeezed gelatine in it. Stir in 4 tablespoons of the coconut cream and then add to the rest of the coconut cream. Fold in the cream and smooth the cream on the chocolate base. Chill for at least 1 hour.*

5. *Roughly chop the dark chocolate and melt it with the coconut oil over a water bath, allow to cool a little. In the meantime, carefully remove the cake from the mould. Cover the cake with the chocolate icing. Sprinkle with the remaining coconut flakes and allow to set. Serve cut into pieces.*

Poppyseed Cheesecake with Coconut

Preparation: 45 min. Ready in 1 h 35 min

Nutritional values

- *Calories 528 kcal (25%)*
- *Protein 17 g (17%)*
- *Fat 29 g (25%)*
- *Carbohydrates 49 g (33%)*
- *added sugar 16.6 g (66%)*
- *Fibre 5.5 g (18%)*

Ingredients

- *100 ml apple juice*

- 80 g dried apricots
- 1 organic lemon
- 200 g butter
- 300 g coconut blossom sugar
- 8 eggs
- 450 g wheat flour type 1050
- 2 tbsp cocoa powder (heavily de-oiled)
- 2 tsp baking powder
- 150 ml milk (3.5% fat)
- 150 g poppy seed baking
- 500 g marzipan paste
- 500 g low-fat quark
- 500 g cream cheese
- 1 tbsp lemon juice
- 1 packet vanilla pudding powder
- 1 pinch salt
- 120 g coconut flakes

Preparation steps

1. Soak apricots in apple juice. Wash lemon with hot water, rub dry, rub peel and squeeze out the juice.
2. For the batter, stir the butter with 150 g coconut blossom sugar and 1 teaspoon lemon zest until creamy and gradually stir in 4 eggs. Mix flour with cocoa and baking powder and fold alternately with milk into the butter and egg mixture. Drain the

apricots, chop them up and mix into the batter with the poppy seeds.

3. Spread half of the batter on a baking sheet lined with baking paper and prebake in a preheated oven at 180 ° C (convection 160 ° C; gas: level 2-3) about 10 minutes.

4. Take out and let cool down.

5. Roll out the marzipan between 2 layers of cling film and cut into wide strips. Lay these on the dough base.

6. Separate the remaining eggs and mix the egg yolks with the quark, cream cheese, remaining coconut blossom sugar, 1 tablespoon lemon juice and vanilla pudding powder. Beat the egg white with a pinch of salt until stiff and fold into the cheese mixture. Spread the mixture on the marzipan, spread the remaining sponge mixture on it, a tablespoon at a time, bake the cake in the hot oven in about 40 minutes, and make a stick test.

7. Take the finished cake out of the oven, let it cool down and sprinkle with coconut flakes.

Chocolate pudding with caramel

Preparation: 30 min. Ready in 1 hour

Nutritional values

- *Calories 521 kcal (25%)*
- *Protein 8 g (8%)*
- *Fat 35 g (30%)*
- *Carbohydrates 45 g (30%)*
- *added sugar 41 g (164%)*
- *Fiber 1.8 g (6%)*

Ingredients

For the cream

- *50 g sugar*
- *1 egg*
- *2 egg yolks*
- *75 g dark chocolate*
- *200 ml of milk*
- *150 ml whipped cream at least 30% fat content*
- *oil for the moulds*

Preparation steps

1. *Beat the sugar with the egg and egg yolks. Roughly chop the chocolate, bring to the boil with the milk and cream in a saucepan and let it flow into the egg mixture while stirring. For the caramel mirror, simmer the sugar with 2 tablespoons of water in a small saucepan until the sugar is golden brown. Immediately pour into the lightly oiled moulds and toss until the caramel is evenly distributed on the moulds' bottom.*

2. *Preheat the oven to an upper and lower heat of 200 ° C. Pour the egg-milk through a sieve and fill the moulds. Place the moulds in a baking dish and fill half of the moulds with boiling water. Let it set in the preheated oven for about 30 minutes. Let the cream cool and turn it out onto a plate to serve.*

Alkaline Blueberry Muffins

Nutrition:

Calories: 160

Fat: 5g

Carbs: 25g

Proteins: 2g

Preparation Time: 5 Minutes

Cooking Time: 20 minutes

Servings: 3

Level of difficulty: Easy

Ingredients:

- 1 cup of coconut milk

- 3/4 cup spelt flour

- *3/4 teff flour*
- *1/2 cup blueberries*
- *1/3 cup agave*
- *1/4 cup sea moss gel*
- *1/2 tsp. sea salt*
- *grapeseed oil*

Directions:

1. *Adjust the temperature of the oven to 365 degrees. Grease 6 regular-size muffin cups with muffin liners.*

2. *In a bowl, mix sea salt, sea moss, agave, coconut milk, and flour gel until they are properly blended. You then crimp in blueberries.*

3. *Coat the muffin pan lightly with the grapeseed oil. Pour in the muffin batter. Bake for at least 30 minutes until it turns golden brown. Serve.*

Coconut Pancakes

Nutrition:

Calories: 377

Fat: 14.9g

Carbs: 60.7g

Protein: 6.4g

Preparation Time: 5 minutes

Cooking Time: 15 minutes

Servings: 4

Level of difficulty: Easy

Ingredients:

- 1 cup coconut flour
- 2 tbsps. arrowroot powder
- 1 tsp. baking powder
- 1 cup of coconut milk

- 3 tbsps. coconut oil

Directions:

1. In a medium container, mix in all the dry ingredients. Add the coconut milk and 2 tbsp of the coconut oil, then mix properly.

2. In a skillet, dissolve 1 tsp of coconut oil. Put the batter into the skillet, then swirl the pan to spread the batter evenly into a smooth pancake.

3. Cook it for like 3 minutes on medium heat until it becomes firm. Turn the pancake to the other side, then cook it for another 2 minutes until it turns golden brown.

4. Cook the remaining pancakes in the same process. Serve.

Sweet Almond Bites

Nutrition:

Calories:
350

Protein: 2

Fat: 38

Carbs: 42g

Preparation Time: 30 minutes

Cooking Time: 2 minutes

Servings: 12

Level of difficulty: Easy

Ingredients:

- *18 ounces butter, grass-fed*

- *2 ounces heavy cream*

- *½ cup stevia*

- *2/3 cup cocoa powder*

- *1 teaspoon vanilla extract, pure*

- *4 tablespoons almond butter*

Directions:

1. *Use a double boiler to dissolve your butter before adding in all of your remaining ingredients. Place the mixture into molds, freezing for two hours before serving.*

Strawberry Cheesecake Minis

Nutrition:

Calories: 372

Protein: 1 g

Fat: 41 g

Carbohydrates: 2 g

Preparation Time: 30 minutes

Cooking Time: 0 minutes

Servings: 12

Level of difficulty: Easy

Ingredients:

- *1 cup of coconut oil*

- *1 cup coconut butter*

- *½ cup strawberries, sliced*

- *½ teaspoon lime juice*

- *2 tablespoons cream cheese, full fat*

- *stevia to taste*

Directions:

1. *Blend your strawberries. Soften your cream cheese, and then add in your coconut butter. Combine all ingredients, and then pour your mixture into silicone molds. Freeze for at least two hours before serving.*

Cocoa Brownies

Nutrition:

Calories: 184

Protein: 1g

Fat: 20g

Carbohydrates:1g

Preparation Time: 10 minutes

Cooking Time: 30 minutes

Level of difficulty: Normal

Servings: 12

Ingredients:

- 1 egg

- 2 tablespoons butter, grass-fed

- *2 teaspoons vanilla extract, pure*

- *¼ teaspoon baking powder*

- *¼ cup of cocoa powder*

- *1/3 cup heavy cream*

- *¾ cup almond butter*

- *pinch sea salt*

Directions:

1. *Break your egg into a bowl, whisking until smooth. Add in all of your wet ingredients, mixing well. Mix all dry ingredients into a bowl.*

2. *Sift your dry ingredients into your wet ingredients, mixing to form a batter. Get out a baking pan, greasing it before pouring in your mixture.*

3. *Warm your oven to 350 F and bake within 25 minutes. Allow it to cool before slicing and serve room temperature or warm.*

Chocolate Orange Bites

Nutrition:

Calories: 188

Protein: 1g

Fat: 21g

Carbohydrates: 5g

Preparation time: 20 minutes

Cooking time: 15 minutes

Servings: 6

Level of difficulty: Normal

Ingredients:

- *10 ounces of coconut oil*

- *4 tablespoons cocoa powder*

- *¼ teaspoon blood orange extract*

- *stevia to taste*

Directions:

1. Melt half of your coconut oil using a double boiler, and then add in your stevia and orange extract.

2. Get out candy molds, pouring the mixture into it. Fill each mold halfway, and then place in the fridge until they set.

3. Melt the other half of your coconut oil, stirring in your cocoa powder and stevia, ensuring that the mixture is smooth with no lumps.

4. Pour into your molds, filling them up all the way, and then allow it to set in the fridge before serving.

Caramel Cones

Nutrition:

Calories: 251

Carbs: 29g

Fat: 13g

Protein: 4g

Preparation Time:25 minutes

Cooking Time: 0 minutes

Servings: 6

Level of difficulty: Easy

Ingredients:

- *2 tablespoons heavy whipping cream*

- *2 tablespoons sour cream*

- *1 tablespoon caramel sugar*

- *1 teaspoon sea salt, fine*

- *1/3 cup butter, grass-fed*

- *1/3 cup coconut oil*

- *stevia to taste*

Directions:

1. *Soften your coconut oil and butter, mixing. Mix all fixings to form a batter, and then places them in molds. Top with a little salt, and keep refrigerated until serving.*

Cinnamon Bites

Nutrition:

Calories:
180

Carbs: 29g

Fat: 6g

Protein: 3g

Preparation Time: 20 minutes

Cooking Time: 5 minutes

Servings: 6

Level of difficulty: Normal

Ingredients:

- 1/8 teaspoon nutmeg

- 1 teaspoon vanilla extract

- ¼ teaspoon cinnamon

- 4 tablespoons coconut oil

- ½ cup butter, grass-fed

- 8 ounces cream cheese

- stevia to taste

Directions:

1. *Soften your coconut oil and butter, mixing in your cream cheese. Add all of your remaining ingredients, and mix well. Pour into molds, and freeze until set.*

Sweet Chai Bites

Nutrition:

Calories: 178

Protein: 1g

Fat: 19g

Carbs: 10g

Preparation Time: 20 minutes

Cooking Time: 45 minutes

Servings: 6

Level of difficulty: Easy

Ingredients:

- 1 cup cream cheese

- 1 cup of coconut oil

- 2 ounces butter, grass-fed

- 2 teaspoons ginger

- 2 teaspoons cardamom

- 1 teaspoon nutmeg

- 1 teaspoon cloves

- 1 teaspoon vanilla extract, pure

- 1 teaspoon Darjeeling black tea

- stevia to taste

Directions:

1. Melt your coconut oil and butter before adding in your black tea. Allow it to sit for one to two minutes.

2. *Add in your cream cheese, removing your mixture from heat. Add in all of your spices, and stir to combine. Pour into molds, and freeze before serving.*

Marinated Eggs

Preparation Time: 2 hours and 10 minutes

Cooking Time: 7 minutes

Servings: 4

Level of difficulty: Normal

Nutrition:

Calories: 289

Protein: 15.86 g

Fat: 22.62 g

Carbohydrates:4.52g

Ingredients:

- *6 eggs*

- *1 and ¼ cups of water*

- *¼ cup unsweetened rice vinegar*

- *2 tablespoons coconut aminos*

- *Salt and black pepper to the taste*

- *2 garlic cloves, minced*

- *1 teaspoon stevia*

- *4 ounces cream cheese*

- *1 tablespoon chives, chopped*

Directions:

1. *Put the eggs in a pot, add water to cover, bring to a boil over medium heat, cover and cook for 7 minutes. Rinse eggs with cold water and leave them aside to cool down.*

2. *In a bowl, mix 1 cup water with coconut aminos, vinegar, stevia, and garlic and whisk well.*

3. *Put the eggs in this mix, cover with a kitchen towel, and leave them aside for 2 hours, rotating from time to time.*

4. *Peel eggs, cut in halves, and put egg yolks in a bowl. Add ¼ cup water, cream cheese, salt, pepper, and chives and stir well. Stuff egg whites with this mix and serve them.*

Chocolate Bars

Nutrition:

Calories: 230

Fat: 24 g

Carbs: 7.5 g

Protein: 6 g

Preparation Time: 10 minutes

Cooking Time: 20 minutes

Servings: 16

Level of difficulty: Normal

Ingredients:

- 15 oz cream cheese, softened

- 15 oz unsweetened dark chocolate

- 1 tsp vanilla

- 10 drops liquid stevia

Directions:

1. Grease an 8-inch square dish and set aside. In a saucepan, dissolve chocolate over low heat. Add stevia and vanilla and stir well.

2. Remove pan from heat and set aside. Add cream cheese into the blender and blend until smooth. Add melted chocolate mixture into the cream cheese and blend until just combined.

3. Transfer mixture into the prepared dish and spread evenly, and place in the refrigerator until firm. Slice and serve.

Blueberry Muffins

Nutrition:

Calories:
190

Fat: 17 g

Carbs: 5 g

Protein: 5 g

Preparation Time: 15 minutes

Cooking Time: 25 minutes

Servings: 12

Level of difficulty: Normal

Ingredients:

- *2 eggs*

- *1/2 cup fresh blueberries*

- *1 cup heavy cream*

- 2 cups almond flour

- 1/4 tsp lemon zest

- 1/2 tsp lemon extract

- 1 tsp baking powder

- 5 drops stevia

- 1/4 cup butter, melted

Directions:

1. Heat the cooker to 350 F. Line muffin tin with cupcake liners and set aside. Add eggs into the bowl and whisk until mix.

2. Add remaining ingredients and mix to combine, then pour the mixture into the prepared muffin tin and bake for 25 minutes. Serve and enjoy.

Chia Pudding

Nutrition:

Calories:
360

Fat: 33 g

Carbs: 13 g

Protein: 6 g

Preparation Time: 20 minutes

Cooking Time: 0 minutes

Servings: 2

Level of difficulty: Easy

Ingredients:

- *4 tbsp chia seeds*

- *1 cup unsweetened coconut milk*

- *1/2 cup raspberries*

Directions:

1. *Add raspberry and coconut milk into a blender and blend until smooth. Pour mixture into the glass jar. Add chia seeds in a jar and stir well.*

2. *Seal the jar with a lid and shake well and place in therefrigerator for 3 hours. Serve chilled and enjoy.*

Avocado Pudding

Nutrition:

Calories: 317

Fat: 30 g

Carbs: 9 g

Protein: 3 g

Preparation Time: 20 minutes

Cooking Time: 0 minutes

Servings: 8

Level of difficulty: Easy

Ingredients:

- *2 ripe avocados, pitted and cut into pieces*

- *1 tbsp fresh lime juice*

- *14 oz coconut milk*

- *2 tsp liquid stevia*

- *2 tsp vanilla*

Directions:

1. *Inside the blender, Add all ingredients and blend until smooth. Serve immediately and enjoy.*

Peanut Butter Coconut Popsicle

Nutrition:

Calories: 155

Fat: 15 g

Carbs: 4 g

Protein: 3 g

Preparation Time: 15 minutes

Cooking Time: 0 minutes

Servings: 12

Level of difficulty: Easy

Ingredients:

- *1/2 cup peanut butter*

- *1 tsp liquid stevia*

- *2 cans unsweetened coconut milk*

Directions:

1. *In the blender, add all the listed ingredients and blend until smooth. Pour mixture into the Popsicle molds and place in the freezer for 4 hours or until set. Serve!*

Delicious Brownie Bites

Nutrition:

Calories: 108

Fat: 9 g

Carbs: 4 g

Protein: 2 g

Preparation Time: 20 minutes

Cooking Time: 0 minutes

Servings: 13

Level of difficulty: Easy

Ingredients:

- 1/4 cup unsweetened chocolate chips

- 1/4 cup unsweetened cocoa powder

- 1 cup pecans, chopped

- 1/2 cup almond butter

- 1/2 tsp vanilla

- 1/4 cup monk fruit sweetener

- 1/8 tsp pink salt

Directions:

1. Add pecans, sweetener, vanilla, almond butter, cocoa powder, and salt into the food processor and process until well combined. Transfer brownie mixture into the large bowl.

2. Add chocolate chips and fold well. Make small round shape balls from brownie mixture and place onto a baking tray. Place in the freezer for 20 minutes. Serve and enjoy.

Pumpkin Balls

Nutrition:

Calories: 96

Fat: 8 g

Carbs: 4 g

Protein: 2 g

Preparation Time: 15 minutes

Cooking Time: 0 minutes

Servings: 18

Level of difficulty: Easy

Ingredients:

- 1 cup almond butter
- 5 drops liquid stevia

- 2 tbsp coconut flour

- 2 tbsp pumpkin puree

- 1 tsp pumpkin pie spice

Directions:

1. Mix pumpkin puree in a large bowl and almond butter until well combined. Add liquid stevia, pumpkin pie spice, and coconut flour and mix well.

2. Make small balls from the mixture and place onto a baking tray in the freezer for 1 hour. Serve and enjoy.

Smooth Peanut Butter Cream

Nutrition:

Calories: 101

Fat: 5 g

Carbs: 14 g

Protein: 3 g

Preparation Time: 10 minutes

Cooking Time: 0 minutes

Servings: 8

Level of difficulty: Easy

Ingredients:

- *1/4 cup peanut butter*

- *4 overripe bananas, chopped*

- *1/3 cup cocoa powder*

- *1/4 tsp vanilla extract*

- *1/8 tsp salt*

Directions:

1. *In the blender, add all the listed ingredients and blend until smooth. Serve immediately and enjoy.*

Vanilla Avocado Popsicles

Nutrition:

Calories: 130

Fat: 12 g

Carbs: 7 g

Protein: 3 g

Preparation Time: 20 minutes

Cooking Time: 0 minutes

Servings: 6

Level of difficulty: Easy

Ingredients:

- *2 avocadoes*

- *1 tsp vanilla*

- *1 cup almond milk*

- *1 tsp liquid stevia*

- *1/2 cup unsweetened cocoa powder*

Directions:

1. *In the blender, add all the listed ingredients and blend smoothly. Pour blended mixture into the Popsicle molds and place in the freezer until set. Serve and enjoy.*

Chocolate Popsicle

Nutrition:

Calories: 198

Fat: 21 g

Carbs: 6 g

Protein: 3 g

Preparation Time: 20 minutes

Cooking Time: 10 minutes

Servings: 6

Level of difficulty: Easy

Ingredients:

- 4 oz unsweetened chocolate, chopped

- 6 drops liquid stevia

- 1 1/2 cups heavy cream

Directions:

1. Add heavy cream into the microwave-safe bowl and microwave until it just begins the boiling. Add chocolate into the heavy cream and set aside for 5 minutes.

2. Add liquid stevia into the heavy cream mixture and stir until chocolate is melted. Pour mixture into the Popsicle molds and place in freezer for 4 hours or until set. Serve and enjoy.

Raspberry Ice Cream

Nutrition:

Calories: 144

Fat: 11 g

Carbs: 10 g

Protein: 2 g

Preparation Time: 10 minutes

Cooking Time: 0 minutes

Servings: 2

Level of difficulty: Easy

Ingredients:

- *1 cup frozen raspberries*

- *1/2 cup heavy cream*

- *1/8 tsp stevia powder*

Directions:

1. *Blend all the listed fixings in a blender until smooth. Serve immediately and enjoy.*

Chocolate Frosty

Nutrition:

Calories: 137

Fat: 13 g

Carbs: 3 g

Protein: 2 g

Preparation Time: 20 minutes

Cooking Time: 0 minutes

Servings: 4

Level of difficulty: Easy

Ingredients:

- *2 tbsp unsweetened cocoa powder*

- *1 cup heavy whipping cream*

- *1 tbsp almond butter*

- *5 drops liquid stevia*

- *1 tsp vanilla*

Directions:

1. *Add cream into the medium bowl and beat using the hand mixer for 5 minutes. Add remaining ingredients and blend until thick cream forms.*

2. *Pour in serving bowls and place them in the freezer for 30 minutes. Serve and enjoy.*

Chocolate Almond Butter Brownie

Nutrition:

Calories: 82

Fat: 2 g

Carbs: 11 g

Protein: 7 g

Preparation Time: 10 minutes

Cooking Time: 16 minutes

Servings: 4

Level of difficulty: Normal

Ingredients:

- 1 cup bananas, overripe

- 1/2 cup almond butter, melted

- 1 scoop protein powder

- 2 tbsp unsweetened cocoa powder

Directions:

1. Warm air fryer to 325 F. Grease air fryer baking pan and set aside. Blend all fixings in a blender until smooth.

2. Pour batter into the prepared pan and place in the air fryer basket, and cook for 16 minutes. Serve and enjoy.

Peanut Butter Fudge

Nutrition:

Calories: 131

Fat: 12 g

Carbs: 4 g

Preparation Time: 10 minutes

Cooking Time: 10 minutes

Servings: 20

Level of difficulty: Normal

Ingredients:

- *1/4 cup almonds, toasted and chopped*

- *12 oz smooth peanut butter*

- 15 drops liquid stevia

- 3 tbsp coconut oil

- 4 tbsp coconut cream

- Pinch of salt

Directions:

1. Line baking tray with parchment paper. Dissolve coconut oil in a pan over low heat. Add peanut butter, coconut cream, stevia, and salt in a saucepan. Stir well.

2. Pour fudge mixture into the prepared baking tray and sprinkle chopped almonds on top. Place the tray in the refrigerator for 1 hour or until set. Slice and serve.

Creamy Raspberry Pomegranate Smoothie

Nutrition:

Calories: 303

fat: 3g

Carbs: 0g

Protein: 15g

Preparation Time: 5 minutes

Cooking Time: 0 minutes

Level of difficulty: Easy

Servings: 1

Ingredients:

- *1½ cups pomegranate juice*

- *½ cup unsweetened coconut milk*

- *1 scoop vanilla protein powder*

- *2 packed cups fresh baby spinach*

- *1 cup frozen raspberries*

- *1 frozen banana*

- *1 to 2 tablespoons freshly compressed lemon juice*

Directions:

1. *In a blender, combine the pomegranate juice and coconut milk. Add the protein powder and spinach. Give these a whirl to break down the spinach.*

2. *Add the raspberries, banana, and lemon juice, then top it off with ice. Blend until smooth and frothy.*

Avocado Kale Smoothie

Nutrition:

Calories: 160

Fat: 13.3g

Carbs: 11.6g

Protein: 2.4g

Preparation Time: 5 minutes

Cooking Time: 0 minutes

Servings: 3

Level of difficulty: Easy

Ingredients:

- 1 cup of water

- ½ Seville orange, peeled

- 1 avocado

- 1 cucumber, peeled

- 1 cup kale

- 1 cup of ice cubes

Directions:

1. Toss all your ingredients into your blender, then process till smooth and creamy. Serve immediately and enjoy.

Apple Kale Cucumber Smoothie

Nutrition:

Calories: 86

Fat: 0.5g

Carbs: 21.7g

Protein: 1.9g

Preparation Time: 5 minutes

Cooking Time: 0 minutes

Servings: 1

Level of difficulty: Easy

Ingredients:

- ¾ *cup of water*

- ½ *green apple, diced*

- ¾ *cup kale*

- ½ *cucumber*

Directions:

1. *Toss all your ingredients into your blender, then process till smooth and creamy. Serve immediately and enjoy.*

Refreshing Cucumber Smoothie

Nutrition:

Calories: 313

Fat: 25.1g

Carbs: 24.7g

Protein: 4.9g

Preparation Time: 5 minutes

Cooking Time: 0 minutes

Servings: 2

Level of difficulty: Easy

Ingredients:

- 1 cup of ice cubes

- 20 drops liquid stevia

- *2 fresh lime, peeled and halved*

- *1 tsp lime zest, grated*

- *1 cucumber, chopped*

- *1 avocado, pitted and peeled*

- *2 cups kale*

- *1 tbsp creamed coconut*

- *¾ cup of coconut water*

Directions:

1. *Toss all your ingredients into your blender, then process till smooth and creamy. Serve immediately and enjoy.*

Cauliflower Veggie Smoothie

Nutrition:

Calories: 71

Fat: 0.3g

Carbs: 18.3g

Protein: 1.3g

Preparation Time: 5 minutes

Cooking Time: 5 minutes

Servings: 4

Level of difficulty: Easy

Ingredients:

- *1 zucchini, peeled and chopped*

- *1 Seville orange, peeled*

- *1 apple, diced*

- *1 banana*

- *1 cup kale*

- *½ cup cauliflower*

Directions:

1. *Toss all your ingredients into your blender, then process till smooth and creamy. Serve immediately and enjoy.*

Soursop Smoothie

Nutrition:

Calories: 213

Fat: 3.1g

Carbs: 6g

Protein: 8g

Preparation Time: 5 minutes

Cooking Time: 0 minutes

Servings: 2

Level of difficulty: Easy

Ingredients:

- *3 quartered frozen Burro Bananas*

- *1-1/2 cups of Homemade Coconut Milk*

- *1/4 cup of Walnuts*

- *1 teaspoon of Sea Moss Gel*

- *1 teaspoon of Ground Ginger*

- *1 teaspoon of Soursop Leaf Powder*

- *1 handful of kale*

Directions:

1. *Prepare and put all ingredients in a blender or a food processor. Blend it well until you reach a smooth consistency. Serve and enjoy your Soursop Smoothie!*

Tiramisu Shake

Preparation time: 5 minutes

Nutrition:

Cooking time: 0 minutes

Calories: 107

Servings: 1

Fat: 0g

Level of difficulty: Easy

Carbohydrates:

15g

Protein: 14g

Ingredients:

- 1 packet Medifast cappuccino mix

- 1 tablespoon sugar-free chocolate syrup

- ½ cup of water

- ½ cup ice, crushed

Directions:

1. In a small blender, place all ingredients and pulse until smooth and creamy. Transfer the shake into a serving glass and serve immediately.

Vanilla Shake

Nutrition:

Calories: 130

Fat: 3.3g

Carbohydrates: 15g

Protein: 13g

Preparation time: 5 minutes

Cooking time: 0 minutes

Servings: 1

Level of difficulty: Easy

Ingredients:

- *½ packet Optavia Vanilla Shake Fueling*

- ½ packet Optavia Gingerbread Fueling

- ½ cup unsweetened almond milk

- ½ cup of water

- 8 ice cubes

Directions:

1. In a small blender, place all ingredients and pulse until smooth. Transfer the smoothie into a serving glass and serve immediately.

Shamrock Shake

Nutrition:

Calories: 120

Fat: 3.9g

Carbohydrates: 13.5g

Protein: 11.7g

Preparation time: 5 minutes

Cooking time: 0 minutes

Servings: 1

Level of difficulty: Easy

Ingredients:

- *1 packet Medifast Vanilla Shake*

- *6 ounces unsweetened almond milk*

- *¼ teaspoon peppermint extract*

- *1-2 drops green food coloring*

- *1 cup of ice cubes*

Directions:

1. *In a small blender, place all ingredients and pulse until smooth. Transfer the smoothie into a serving glass and serve immediately.*

Coconut Smoothie

Nutrition:

Calories: 120

Fat: 6.2g

Preparation time: 5 minutes

Cooking time: 0 minutes

Servings: 1

Carbohydrates:
15.9g

Protein: 15g

Level of difficulty: Easy

Ingredients:

- 1 sachet Optavia Essential Creamy Vanilla Shake

- 6 ounces unsweetened almond milk

- *6 ounces diet ginger ale*

- *2 tablespoons unsweetened coconut, shredded*

- *¼ teaspoon rum extract*

- *½ cup ice*

Directions:

1. *In a small blender, place all ingredients and pulse until smooth. Transfer the smoothie into a serving glass and serve immediately.*

Vanilla Frappe

Nutrition:

Calories: 155

Fat: 4.4g

Carbohydrates:
15.2g

Protein: 15g

Preparation time: 5 minutes

Cooking time: 0 minutes

Servings: 1

Level of difficulty: Easy

Ingredients:

- 1 sachet Optavia Essential Vanilla Shake

- 8 ounces unsweetened almond milk

- ½ cup ice

- 1 tablespoon whipped topping

Directions:

1. In a blender, add the Vanilla Shake sachet, almond milk, and ice and pulse until smooth. Transfer the mixture into a glass and top with whipped topping. Serve immediately.

Pumpkin Frappe

Nutrition:

Calories: 138

Fat: 4.8g

Carbohydrates: 16.4g

Protein: 11.7g

Preparation time: 5 minutes

Cooking time: 0 minutes

Servings: 1

Level of difficulty: Easy

Ingredients:

- *1 sachet Optavia Essential Spiced Gingerbread*

- *4 ounces strong brewed coffee*

- *4 ounces unsweetened almond milk*

- 1/8 teaspoon pumpkin pie spice

- ½ cup ice

- 1 tablespoon whipped topping

Directions:

1. In a blender, add the Spiced Gingerbread sachet, coffee, almond milk, pumpkin pie spice, and ice and pulse until smooth. Transfer the mixture into a glass and top with whipped topping. Serve immediately.

Chocolate Frappe

Nutrition:

Calories: 148

Fat: 4.8g

Carbohydrates: 18g

Protein: 11.7g

Preparation time: 5 minutes

Cooking time: 0 minutes

Servings: 1

Level of difficulty: Easy

Ingredients:

- *1 sachet Optavia Essential Frosty Mint Chocolate Soft Serve Treat*

- *4 ounces strong brewed coffee*

- *4 ounces unsweetened almond milk*

- *1½ tablespoons sugar-free chocolate syrup, divided*

- *¼ teaspoon peppermint extract*

- *½ cup ice*

- *1 tablespoon whipped topping*

Directions:

1. *In a blender, add the Chocolate sachet, coffee, almond milk, 1 tablespoon of chocolate syrup, peppermint extract, and ice and pulse until smooth.*

2. *Transfer the mixture into a glass and top with whipped topping. Drizzle with remaining chocolate syrup and serve immediately.*

Peppermint Mocha Shake

Nutrition:

Calories: 133

Fat: 1.1g

Carbohydrates: 15.2g

Protein: 14.6g

Preparation time: 5 minutes

Cooking time: 0 minutes

Servings: 1

Level of difficulty: Easy

Ingredients:

- *1 sachet Optavia Essential Velvety Hot Chocolate*

- *6 ounces freshly brewed coffee*

- *¼ cup warm unsweetened almond milk*

- *¼ teaspoon peppermint extract*

- *One tablespoon whipped topping*

- *Pinch of ground cinnamon*

Directions:

1. *In a serving mug, place the Hot Chocolate sachet, coffee, almond milk, and peppermint extract and stir until well blended.*

2. *Top the hot chocolate with whipped topping and sprinkle with cinnamon. Serve immediately.*

Thanks again for choosing this book, make sure to leave a short review on amazon if you enjoy it, I would really love to hear your thoughts.